# ISAAC ASIMOV'S
## Library of the Universe

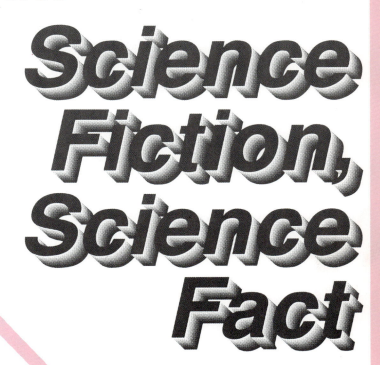

**Science Fiction, Science Fact**

by Isaac Asimov

Gareth Stevens Publishing
Milwaukee

**Library of Congress Cataloging-in-Publication Data**

Asimov, Isaac, 1920-
    Science fiction, science fact.

    (Isaac Asimov's Library of the universe)
    Bibliography:   p.
    Includes index.
    Summary:  Compares what writers over the centuries have written about an imaginary future with the reality revealed by time.
    1. Science—Juvenile literature.   2. Science fiction—Juvenile literature.
[1. Science fiction—History and criticism.   2. Forecasting.   I. Title.   II.
Series:  Asimov, Isaac, 1920-    .  Library of the universe.
Q163.A86    1989                     500                    87-42591
ISBN 1-55532-323-5


A Gareth Stevens Children's Books edition

Edited, designed, and produced by
Gareth Stevens, Inc.
RiverCenter Building, Suite 201
1555 North RiverCenter Drive
Milwaukee, Wisconsin  53212, USA

Cover art © Al Gutierrez
Project editor:  Mark Sachner
Designer:  Laurie Shock
Research editor:  Scott Enk
Picture research:  Matthew Groshek
Technical advisers and consulting editors:  Julian Baum and Francis Reddy

    3 4 5 6 7 8 9 94 93 92 91 90

**Printed in the United States of America**

# CONTENTS

Nowadays, we have seen planets up close, all the way to distant Uranus. We have mapped Venus through its clouds. We have seen dead volcanoes on Mars and live ones on Io, Jupiter's satellite. We have detected strange objects no one knew anything about until recently: quasars, pulsars, black holes. We have learned amazing facts about how the Universe was born and have some ideas about how it may die. Nothing can be more astonishing and more interesting.

Still, long before any of these discoveries were made, writers wondered what the future would hold, what strange discoveries might be made, what new things we might learn about the Universe. It was very difficult for these science fiction writers, despite their excellent imaginations, to guess just <u>how</u> strange the Universe was. Still, they sometimes made remarkably good guesses. Let's compare science fiction and science fact.

*Isaac Asimov*

## The Visionaries

For centuries — even in ancient Roman times — writers have imagined people traveling to the Moon.  By the 1800s, however, what we call the Industrial Revolution was under way.  People saw how inventions were changing the world with machines, and writers imagined more and more just how machines might change our lives in years to come.  For example, a French science fiction writer, Jules Verne, wrote of advanced submarines, and of a spaceship shot to the Moon by a cannon — from Florida!

An English science fiction writer, H. G. Wells, in a story called *The War in the Air*, described in 1908 the bombing of cities from the air.  In *The World Set Free*, written in 1914, he wrote about atomic bombs. In his 1901 story *The First Men in the Moon*, Wells had people float to the Moon in a ship that canceled gravity.

Opposite and above: In the first science fiction movie, *A Trip to the Moon*, a giant cannon fires a bulletlike ship right into the eye of our nearest neighbor. The movie was made in 1902.

**Will the <u>real</u> first science fiction story please stand up?**

*How old is science fiction? Some people think Homer's* Odyssey *is science fiction; others say it is only fantasy. Some say you can't have science fiction unless you base it on new developments in science. They think* Frankenstein *is the first science fiction story; others say it's only gothic romance. Some say you need solid science in your story and that* Five Weeks in a Balloon *is the first science fiction story. This dispute will probably never be settled.*

October

⬥BROADCAST⬥
WRNY
STATION

25 CENTS

# AMAZING STORIES

HUGO GERNSBACK
EDITOR

Stories by-
H·G·Wells
Ray Cummings
Garret Smith

EXPERIMENTER PUBLISHING COMPANY, NEW YORK, PUBLISHERS OF
RADIO NEWS · SCIENCE & INVENTION · RADIO LISTENERS' GUIDE · SPARE-TIME MONEY MAKING · FRENCH HUMOR

## Predicting the Future

In 1926, *Amazing Stories*, the first magazine devoted entirely to science fiction, appeared. From then on, more and more writers described space travel. They generally used rockets, the one method we have discovered that really works. They traveled not only to the Moon in their stories, but to all the planets and their satellites.

In 1928, one exciting story, "The Skylark of Space," even described voyages to other stars. Sometimes other planets were described as being inhabited by hostile aliens. Mars, long thought to be a possible home for life beyond Earth, was often treated as a dangerous threat to Earth.

Opposite: Humans meet aliens on the cover of this 1927 magazine.

Right: Flying saucers aren't a recent phenomenon — just look at this magazine cover from 1918!

Below: In this 1928 magazine, a lion gets a surprise when he tries to make a meal of a robot.

**The future right before your very eyes — some modern predictions**

*Sometimes writers make lucky guesses. In 1941, Robert A. Heinlein wrote a story. In it, he described something like the "Manhattan Project" and the invention of the atomic bomb, which came after the story was published. Isaac Asimov wrote stories about robots 40 years before they were developed. He was the first to use the word "robotics," which is now in common use. He also described the pocket computer in 1950, some 20 years before it came into use.* •

# You Can't Hurry Space Travel

Of course, now, a century after Jules Verne, we can see where science fiction writers guessed wrong. Most described rocket ships zipping across the Solar system as though they were airplanes going from New York to Los Angeles. Actually, it takes rockets months to coast to Mars and years to reach the distant outer planets.

If rockets kept their engines firing, they could go a little faster. But in real life, rockets simply can't carry enough fuel to do that for long. In real life, you can only carry so much fuel, and in real life you would be able to make it do only so much.

In 1638, *The Man in the Moon*, by Francis Godwin, was published. The story concerns a man whose trained geese go out of control and fly him to the moon!

### Rockets win the space race — by a nose

Rockets are the only way we can get people and instruments into space. The English scientist Isaac Newton first explained the law by which rockets work. But the first person to actually suggest rockets for space travel was a science fiction writer, Cyrano de Bergerac (the one with the nose — yes, he really lived). He mentioned rockets in his 1656 novel about a Moon voyage. He also mentioned six other ways to reach the Moon — none of which would ever work. ●

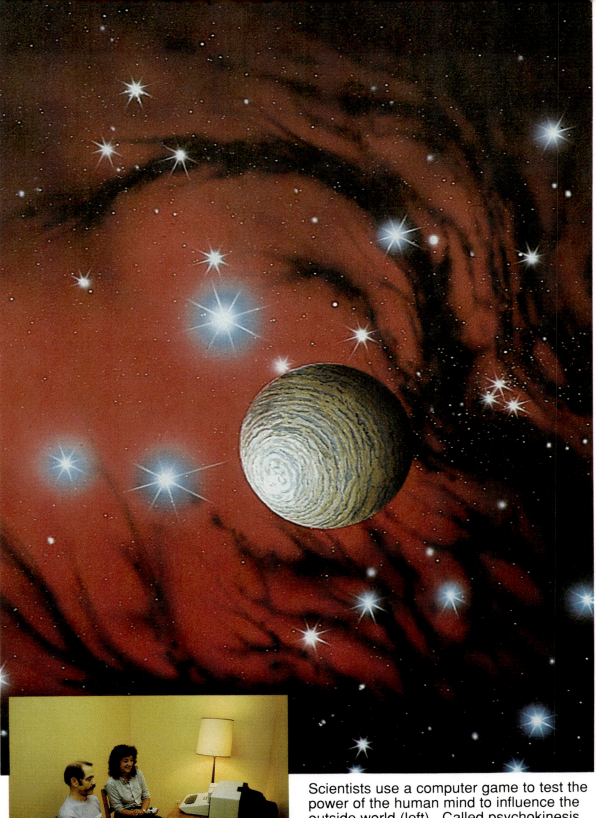

Scientists use a computer game to test the power of the human mind to influence the outside world (left). Called psychokinesis, this as-yet-unproven ability may one day power spaceships to the remote reaches of space (above) — as some science fiction writers have suggested.

# People in Space — The Reality

In early science fiction stories, people on spaceships were usually pictured as leading normal lives, just as if they were on ocean liners. The writers knew that spaceships coasting through space would experience zero gravity, or weightlessness, but most just assumed that there would be some sort of artificial gravity.

In reality, astronauts on real spaceships, so far at least, have had to live with weightlessness. This introduces certain difficulties, but one Soviet cosmonaut lived almost two-thirds of a year in the weightlessness of space.

Both the cosmonaut aboard Mir (above) and the astronaut aboard Skylab — the largest space station yet placed in orbit (opposite) — had to put up with weightlessness and cramped living conditions.

In these scenes from "Star Trek," occupants of the USS Enterprise, a 23rd-century starship, live with plenty of room and the sensation of gravity.

A scene from *First Men in the Moon*, a 1964 movie based on a story by H. G. Wells. United Nations astronauts are surprised to find a British flag and other evidence of earlier Moon visitors.

## Men on the Moon

Naturally, science fiction writers want their stories to be exciting. But as we see in stories about trips to the Moon, making a story more exciting doesn't always make it more accurate.

Jules Verne just described the trip itself and didn't have his heroes land on the Moon. That wasn't exciting enough. H. G. Wells's heroes landed on the Moon, and for more excitement, they encountered an advanced civilization.

But the Moon in fact has not been like the Moon in fiction. When human beings actually did land on the Moon in 1969, they found no civilization. The Moon was a completely dead world.

But when the landing was made, hundreds of millions of people on Earth watched it on television. That was <u>one</u> scientific achievement the early science fiction writers hadn't thought of — watching a Moon landing on television!

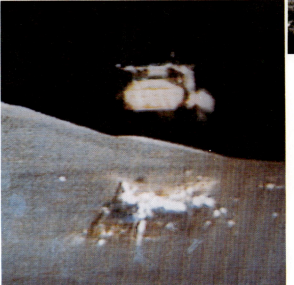

Above: Astronaut Edwin "Buzz" Aldrin poses near a US flag left on the Moon by the Apollo 11 crew in 1969.

Right: a wonder of science fact — television pictures from the Moon. A camera remotely controlled from Houston made it possible for people on Earth to watch this spectacular liftoff from the Moon's surface in 1972.

# Living in Space — Fact or Fantasy?

Early science fiction writers assumed that all the planets were fairly Earth-like. Settlers on Venus would hunt dinosaurs. There would be grain fields on Mars, irrigated by water from the canals. And as scientists learned that planetary atmospheres were not breathable, the writers invented domed or underground cities with special atmospheres.

If we want to explore or settle other parts of the Solar system, we may have to do something like this someday. Better still, we might build artificial worlds in space with Earth-like environments. Few science fiction writers ever thought of that.

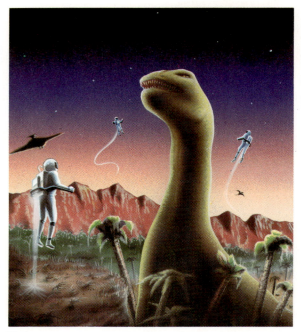

This scene could be from an imaginary visit to Venus or to prehistoric Earth.

In his 1726 book *Gulliver's Travels* Jonathan Swift invented the floating island of Laputa.

---

### Two satellites for Mars: Swift — and lucky — guesswork

*In* Gulliver's Travels, *Jonathan Swift wrote about a fictional land where astronomy was very advanced. In that land, astronomers discovered that Mars had two small satellites. The book was written in 1726. No such satellites were known then, but a little over 150 years later two satellites were discovered orbiting Mars pretty much as Swift had described. Swift had made a lucky guess, but it was based on the ideas of scientist Johannes Kepler.* ●

A factory of the future?  On Umbriel, a moon of Uranus, explorers set up a chemical refinery.

Current US plans call for the construction of a giant space station, called Freedom, in the 1990s. Soviet space pioneer Konstantin Tsiolkovsky wrote about space stations in the 1920s.

## Working in Space — Fantasy Becomes Fact

In order to live in space, we will have to work in space. And to do that we will first have to build a space station close to Earth. It would be a place where people could permanently live, work, and put together new spaceships for exploration farther out in space.

Space stations were described in a 1920 science fiction story by Soviet rocket scientist Konstantin Tsiolkovsky. Since the 1950s, scientists have designed space stations as great spinning wheels. The spin would produce effects resembling gravity. Space stations haven't been built yet, and when they are, they will probably be smaller and simpler than those that have been imagined.

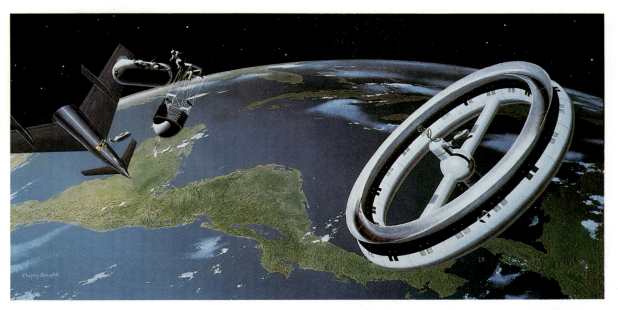

In 1951, scientist Wernher von Braun and artist Chesley Bonestell predicted a piloted mission to Mars. They described a reusable space vehicle, a space station, and even an orbiting telescope (top picture). A more recent NASA illustration featuring a space shuttle, space station, and observation satellite (bottom) shows that their prediction was on target!

# Galactic Civilizations?

In order to make their stories more exciting, science fiction writers often imagine different forms of life on various planets. Usually, the writers include advanced, intelligent life forms that might often be hostile to humans.

Sometimes, the writers of books, films, and television shows imagine that different forms of life join some sort of confederation or political union. We often hear about a "Galactic Federation" or even a "Galactic Empire."

In reality, we have no actual evidence — at least not yet — that <u>any</u> life exists beyond Earth. But still we dream of seeking — and finding — advanced life forms among the stars.

Opposite: Space probes descend from a giant ship to explore a strange new world.

As Earth civilization expands into space, we may run into other civilizations. Perhaps we'll even be invited to join a Galactic Federation made up of different life forms in the Milky Way.

19

## Star Travel —
## Breaking the Laws of Nature

The idea of star travel is appealing — but it's not very realistic! For instance, if there were a Galactic Empire, how do you think its members would communicate? And how would people travel from one star to the next? Ever since 1905, scientists have known that nothing we know of can possibly go faster than the speed of light, which travels at 186,000 miles (300,000 km) a second. And as fast as that is, it is not a speed at which humans could ever travel.

Science fiction writers are forced to break the laws of nature and imagine something like "hyperspace" through which spaceships can go faster than light — like taking a shortcut through a long, long wall, instead of having to march to the very end and back.

An artist's conception of a starship traveling at nearly the speed of light. To the crew, both the time and the distance traveled would pass normally, although the Universe would appear vastly different. But if we could observe such a trip from Earth, the time and distance passed by such a ship would seem enormous. In fact, we would grow old much more quickly than the crew.

## Star Travel — The Reality

Scientists feel quite certain that there is no getting around the speed-of-light limit. That's why there would be little real chance of a Galactic Empire. Even if there are many intelligent civilizations in the Galaxy, each will probably remain isolated from the others. Those who someday explore the Galaxy will find it a long, slow process in which different settlements would become isolated.

Some say that since there is no real proof that intelligent beings from outer space have visited us, no such beings are out there. Perhaps there are, but the odds are very, very small that they would find us in the vastness of space.

Inset, opposite: the Arecibo Message of 1974. The message describes life on Earth to other possible civilizations in space. Actually beamed toward a distant star cluster in the Milky Way, the message includes a human figure (♀), a diagram of our Solar system (⚊⚊⚊), and an image of the radio telescope at Arecibo, Puerto Rico, that beamed the message (⌂).

Opposite: The Arecibo Message is received and decoded by joyful alien life forms thousands of years after its transmission.

Left: A radio-telescope receiver on a distant world scans the skies for messages from other civilizations.

## We Live in Their Future

Science fiction writers of the past usually underestimated how fast things change.

In 1900, most writers who visualized air flight thought of advanced dirigibles, or of small airplanes capable of carrying only one or two people. When they imagined rocket ships going to the Moon, they didn't think of all the myriad ways in which we put space to use. Back then, most didn't think of communications satellites, weather satellites, or navigational satellites.

But they <u>did</u> think of space suits very much like those that real astronauts have used. They also imagined things like television, microfilm, tape recorders, lasers, and even charge cards. On a lot of things, science fiction writers of long ago <u>were</u> right!

Opposite, above: a rocket belt in its most modern form — the manned maneuvering unit (MMU) — is put through its first run outside the Earth-orbiting shuttle Challenger in 1984.

Opposite, below: an early fictional version of the rocket belt. In 1649, Cyrano de Bergerac wrote *Voyage to the Moon*, the story of a man who straps bottles of morning dew to his waist and uses the power of evaporation to float upward. But instead of reaching the Moon, he lands in Canada!

Unrestrained by the bulky trappings of the MMU, this rocket belt whisks its comic book hero away from the clutches of villains below.

### Science fiction's popularity — what's the big deal?

For years, science fiction writers had a lot of fun writing their stories, but did not make much money. Then, in the 1980s, they became "big time." Why? It's hard to say. Some people think the world has become "science fictiony." Computers, robots, and trips to the Moon have put people in a science fiction mood. Others say that blockbuster science fiction movies have made people interested. Whatever it is, it has made science fiction writers happy. •

**?**

# War in Space — Let's Hope It Stays Fiction

Science fiction writers often envisioned war in space, but they tended to imagine air battles. The spaceships maneuvered rapidly and shot each other down with disintegrator rays. We still see that in science fiction movies.

In real life, the disintegrator rays have become laser beams manipulated by computers. In their imaginary view of war in space, science fiction writers weren't much good at imagining computers!

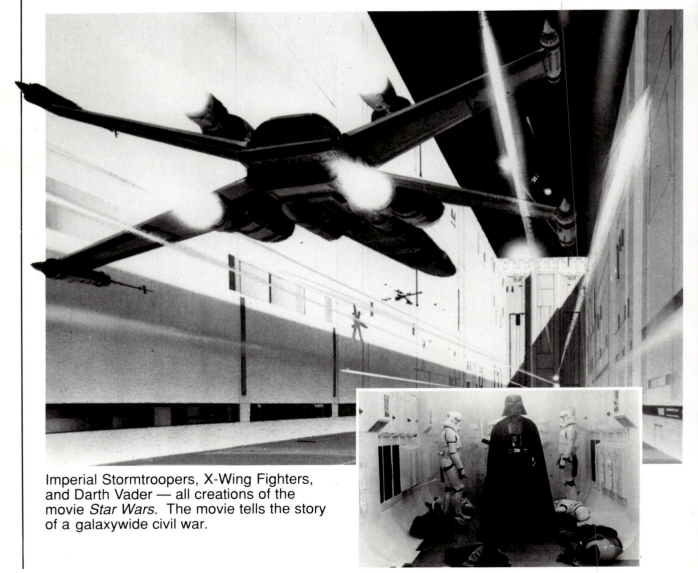

Imperial Stormtroopers, X-Wing Fighters, and Darth Vader — all creations of the movie *Star Wars*. The movie tells the story of a galaxywide civil war.

Despite some of the differences between science fact and fiction, real war in space could match or surpass fictional wars in one way — the terrible power to destroy our planet. How sad that would be! Surely that is not why we have ventured into space.

And surely that would be a tragic way for science fiction to predict science fact.

Below: So far, no war has ever been fought in space. But weapons designed to destroy satellites have been tested by both the US and the Soviet Union.

Left: A war fought in space could devastate our fragile planet.

# Fact File:  Sometimes, Science Fiction <u>Becomes</u> Science Fact

Science fiction writers love to predict the future.  It might seem that many things described in science fiction — travel to other galaxies and time travel, for instance — are just impossible, or won't exist until way in the future.

But many things that science fiction writers of long ago wrote about really do exist today — sometimes years, or even centuries, before even <u>they</u> thought their ideas would become reality!

## MODERN INVENTIONS THAT WERE ONCE THE DREAMS OF SCIENCE FICTION WRITERS

| INVENTION | PREDICTED BY | DATE ACTUALLY INVENTED |
|---|---|---|
| Air-conditioned skyscrapers | Jules Verne, *In the Twenty-Ninth Century — The Day of an American Journalist* (1875) | 1930 |
| Artificial intelligence (including computers that can "think" for themselves) | Ammianus Marcellinus (Aaron Nadel), "The Thought Machine," *Amazing Stories* magazine (1927) | 1950s-present |
| Atomic energy | H. G. Wells, *The World Set Free* (1914) | 1942 |
| Charge cards | Edward Bellamy, *Looking Backward, 2000-1887* (1888) | 1952 |
| Lasers | Sir Francis Bacon (1626) | 1960 |
| Long-distance submarines | Jules Verne, *Twenty Thousand Leagues Under the Sea* (1870) | 1950s-present |
| Microfilm | Hugo Gernsback, *Ralph 124C 41+* (1911) | 1920 |
| Navigational satellites | Edward Everett Hale (1870) | 1959 |

For instance, most people in the 1800s probably thought that the inventions we call television, air-conditioned skyscrapers, and spacecraft were far-off dreams. But these — and many other dreams of science fiction writers of long ago — are everyday parts of modern life. Sometimes, fiction <u>does</u> become fact!

| INVENTION | PREDICTED BY | DATE ACTUALLY INVENTED |
|---|---|---|
| News broadcasts | Jules Verne, *In the Twenty-Ninth Century* (1875) | 1920 |
| Robots | Karel Capek, *R. U. R.* ("Rossum's Universal Robots") (1921) | 1920s-present |
| Spacesuits | Frank R. Paul, *Amazing Stories* magazine (1939) | 1950s and 1960s |
| Spacecraft that could carry people to the Moon | Jules Verne, *From the Earth to the Moon* (1865) H. G. Wells, *The First Men in the Moon* (1901) | 1960s |
| Tape recorders | Hugo Gernsback, *Ralph 124C 41+* (1911) | 1936 |
| Television | Jules Verne, *In the Twenty-Ninth Century* (1875) H. G. Wells, *The Time Machine* (1895) | 1920s |
| Test-tube babies | Aldous Huxley, *Brave New World* (1931) | 1978 |

# More Books About Science Fiction

Here is a list of books that contain science fiction or information about science fiction. If you are interested in them, check your library or bookstore.

*The Donkey Planet.* Corbett (Dutton)
*The First Men in the Moon.* Wells (Airmont)
*I Was a Second Grade Werewolf.* Pinkwater (Live Oak Media)
*Meet E. T. the Extra-Terrestrial.* Klimo (Simon & Schuster)
*Star Trek: Voyage into Adventure.* Dodge (Archway)
*The War of the Worlds.* Wells (Putnam)

# Places to Visit

### For science fiction
Here is a home museum that has one of the world's largest collections of science fiction literature and artwork, including posters and souvenirs of science fiction movies. It is open to the public most Saturday afternoons.

The Fantasy Foundation
Forrest J Ackerman's Archive of the Fantastic
2495 Glendower Avenue
Hollywood, California 90027

To phone ahead, dial
(213) MOONFAN
(213-666-6326)

Most towns, especially larger cities and towns with colleges and universities, have libraries and bookstores with collections of science fiction. Also, many cities have used and rare book shops, as well as new and used comic book shops. These shops often carry a wide selection of science fiction.

### For science fact
Here are some museums where you can explore the wonders of scientific achievement, including inventions that have made space exploration possible.

Ontario Science Centre
Toronto, Ontario

Junior Museum
San Francisco, California

Edmonton Space Sciences Centre
Edmonton, Alberta

Museum of Science and Industry
Chicago, Illinois

Mitchell Gallery of Flight
Mitchell International Airport
Milwaukee, Wisconsin

National Air and Space Museum
Smithsonian Institution
Washington, DC

## For More Information About Science Fiction

Here are some people you can write to for more information and answers to your questions about science fiction. Be sure to tell them your age and exactly what you want to know about or see. To be sure of a reply, enclose a self-addressed, stamped envelope.

Los Angeles Science Fantasy Society
11513 Burbank Boulevard
North Hollywood, California 91601

Baltimore Science Fiction Society, Inc.
P. O. Box 686
Baltimore, Maryland 21203

# Glossary

*aliens:* in this book, beings from some place other than Earth.

*artificial:* imitation; manufactured by people instead of occurring in nature.

*astronomy:* the scientific study of the Universe and its various bodies.

*atmosphere:* the gases surrounding a planet, star, or moon.

*atomic bomb:* a bomb that gets its power from the energy released when atoms under great pressure fuse or divide. When this enormously destructive device explodes, its blast can kill all forms of life both right away and more slowly, through the release of radiation which causes illness.

*black hole:* an object in space caused by the explosion and collapse of a star. This object is so tightly packed that not even light can escape the force of its gravity.

*cosmonaut:* an astronaut, especially one from the Soviet Union.

*Cyrano de Bergerac:* (pronounced SIR-ah-no deh BUR-jeh-rack) a French writer known for his plays and fantasies — and his long nose. He was also used as a fictional character by writer Edmond Rostand.

*dirigible:* an airship consisting of a balloon and a hold for engine and passengers. The balloon is filled with hydrogen and helium gases to make it lighter than air.

*disintegrator ray:* an imaginary weapon that shoots a beam, breaking the target into fragments or turning it into vapor.

*gothic romance:* a story which is about a love affair and which contains elements that are bizarre, mysterious, or ghostly.

*Industrial Revolution:* the change from a society that is based mainly on agriculture, or farming, to one based on manufacturing goods with machinery, on a large scale, as in factories.

*irrigate:* to supply dry land with water through ditches, pipes, or streams.

*Kepler, Johannes:* a German astronomer who lived from 1571 to 1630. He calculated a pattern of moons for the known planets of his day ranging from none for Venus to one for Earth, one or two for Mars, and four for Jupiter.

*laser beam:* a powerful ray of light that can be both precisely focused and intense enough to burn holes through the hardest materials known. Lasers are currently used for delicate surgery and for cutting gems.

*Manhattan Project:* code name for a group of scientists working in the United States to produce an atomic bomb during World War II.

*probe:* a craft that travels in space, photographing celestial bodies and even landing on some of them.

*pulsar:* a star with all the mass of an ordinary large star but with that mass squeezed into a small ball. It sends out rapid pulses of light or electrical waves.

*quasar:* a "quasi-stellar," or "star-like," core of a galaxy that may have a large black hole at its center.

*radio telescope:* an instrument that uses a radio receiver and antenna to both see into space and to listen for messages from space.

*robotics:* the study and making of robots, which are mechanical devices that can perform certain human tasks.

*satellite:* a smaller body orbiting a larger body. The Moon is Earth's <u>natural</u> satellite. Communication, weather, and navigational satellites are examples of <u>artificial</u> satellites.

# Index

The publishers wish to thank the following for permission to reproduce copyright material: front cover, pp. 15, 18, © Alan Gutierrez; pp. 4, 5, 26 (both), 28 (lower), The Museum of Modern Art Film Stills Archive; pp. 6, 7 (both), 28 ("Ralph" cover), from the collection of Sam Moskowitz; pp. 8, 25 (lower), © Lee Bataglia; p. 9 (lower), © Institute for Parapsychology; pp. 10, 16, Oberg Archives; pp. 11 (upper), 13 (both), 25 (upper), photographs courtesy of NASA; p. 11 (both lower), Photofest; p. 12, The Kobal Collection; p. 14 (upper), © Sal Erato, 1988; p. 14 (lower), courtesy of Griffith Observatory; p. 17 (upper), © Chesley Bonestell/Space Art International; p. 17 (lower), courtesy of McDonnell Douglas; p. 19, © Julian Baum; pp. 20-21, 23 (large), © Mark Paternostro, 1988; p. 22, © David A. Hardy; p. 23 (inset), National Astronomy and Ionosphere Center/Cornell University; p. 24, Art by Matthew Groshek, © Gareth Stevens, Inc., 1988; p. 27 (upper), courtesy of Los Alamos National Laboratory; p. 28 (computer/money card), © Jon Feingersch/Tom Stack and Associates, 1988; p. 29 (upper), © Steve Elmore/Tom Stack and Associates, 1986; p. 29 (center right), © Claude Charlier/Science Source/Photo Researchers.